Henry Aaron

Dream Chaser

Roz Morris

Seacoast Publishing
Birmingham, Alabama

Henry Aaron: Dream Chaser

Published by Seacoast Publishing, Inc.
1149 Mountain Oaks Drive
Birmingham, Alabama 35226

Library of Congress Control Number: 2001096681

Cover art and text illustrations by Thomas B. Moore

ISBN 1-878561-94-4

To obtain copies of this book, please write or call:
Seacoast Publishing, Inc.
Post Office Box 26492
Birmingham, Alabama 35260
(205) 979-2909

Dedication

To Drew, for love of the game.

About The Series

Alabama Roots is a book series designed to provide reading pleasure for young people, to allow readers to better know the men and women who shaped the State of Alabama, and to fill a much-needed void of quality regional non-fiction for students in middle grades.

For years, teachers and librarians have searched for quality biographies about famous people from Alabama. This series is a response to that search. The series will cover a span of time from pre-statehood through the modern day.

The goal of *Alabama Roots* is to provide biographies that are historically accurate and as interesting as the characters whose lives they explore.

The *Alabama Roots* mark assures readers and educators of consistent quality in research, composition, and presentation.

It is a joint publishing project of Seacoast Publishing, Inc., and Will Publishing, Inc., both located in Birmingham, Alabama.

Photographs in this book are from the Aaron family collection. Some hang on the walls of Estella Aaron's home in Mobile, where Henry grew up. Mrs. Aaron graciously allowed a photographer to come to her home and make copies of the photos.

Roz Morris

On February 27, 1914, the 19-year-old son of a Baltimore, Maryland, bartender signed a contract to play baseball for his hometown team, the Orioles.

He had learned the game at St. Mary's Industrial School for Boys, a combination reform school and orphanage.

It was a game that he liked. In fact, it was a game that he played better than anyone else at St. Mary's.

After the Orioles, he played in Boston and New York. Before he was through he had done things that no other baseball player had ever done.

Some said they were things that no one would ever do again.

His name was George Herman Ruth.

Babe Ruth.

The New York fans loved Babe. So many came just to see him play at Yankee Stadium, the ballpark was nicknamed The House That Ruth Built.

He was the first great home-run hitter in baseball.

By the end of his baseball playing days in 1935, he had hit 714 home runs—the most that any player had ever hit in the history of the game.

Many people thought the record would never be broken.

None of them had ever heard of Henry Louis Aaron.

Prologue

HENRY AARON STARED miserably toward the baseball diamond at Carver Park.

It was the cause of his problems. At that moment, big problems.

It was also his greatest pleasure in life.

He had gotten caught doing something he was not supposed to do. And it had a lot to do with the game he played so well at Carver Park. Was he mad for getting caught? Or upset by it? Was there regret? Or only resentment?

He was battling mixed emotions as he turned to look into his father's reproachful eyes.

"Come on, Man, let's sit in the car out in front of the house and talk," his father ordered, gently, but in a way that he knew he better do it.

Henry nodded and slowly walked toward the old car parked in front of his house. He knew he deserved to be punished by his Daddy. He knew that his mother and father were disappointed in him. They taught him to do the best that he could, no matter what the job. Mama always told him he should be able to look in the mirror and say, "I gave it all that I've got."

Deep in his heart, Henry knew he had not done that.

The trouble started that morning at school. Everyone was in the gym listening to the principal, Dr. Benjamin Baker, just like they did every Monday morning.

Dr. Baker made a point to single out a boy at each assembly. It always was to talk about something the boy had done wrong. It seemed like Dr. Baker thought that embarrassing students would make them behave better.

This morning, Henry tried to make himself invisible in the back of the gym.

But, as the sun glinted from the dusty windows into his eyes, his heart fell. Dr. Baker was pointing right at him and calling his name. Henry knew he was about to get it. His normally swift feet felt like lead as he shuffled across the gym floor.

Dr. Baker ranted and raved in front of the whole school about Henry being absent so many days. He whacked Henry with his cane! Yet, none of that hurt nearly as much as what Dr. Baker said next.

"I want you to go home and get your father so he can give me a reason for why you have missed all of these days!" Dr. Baker bellowed.

Those words terrified

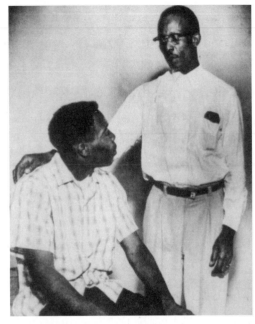

Young Henry with his father

Henry. He knew that telling his father was going to be the hardest thing he'd ever done.

He had been taking the coins that his father left him for a school lunch each day and using them to play pool while he listened to the Dodgers on the radio instead of going to school.

Mama had her heart set on Henry going to college. She wanted her son to be a school teacher. He knew she was going to be upset when she found out he had been skipping school—especially for baseball.

Suddenly, he realized that he and his father and

been sitting in the car in silence for a long time. He looked over to his father.

"Man, what were you thinking?" Daddy asked. "What were you doing?"

The boy just shook his head.

"Mama and I aren't going to let you quit school," Daddy continued.

"Every morning I put a quarter on the table so you can go to school and have a good lunch," Daddy said. "I only take one quarter with me to work (where food costs more) because your education is more important than my stomach."

"I know that, Daddy, and I do appreciate all that you do.

"But, Daddy, what does it matter?" he challenged, "I'm going to be a ball player."

Henry Aaron was chasing a dream.

It was a dream that would not go away.

But for a skinny 15-year-old kid on a poor street in Mobile, Alabama, it would have to wait.

Henry's Mama and Daddy took him out of Dr. Baker's school and enrolled him in a private school.

His baseball dreams came in second to their dreams of his going to school.

1

WILCOX COUNTY LIES in the heart of Alabama's black belt, a strip of dark earth that stretches east and west across the state south of Montgomery where cotton grows in broad fields.

It was a place where the sons of plantation owners and the sons of former slaves still planted cotton, just like their fathers and grandfathers before them.

They lived in the same country villages, but not usually on the same streets. The white people had their part of town, and the black people had theirs.

That is the way it was in Camden, the county seat of Wilcox County, just east of the Alabama River.

Herbert Aaron lived in Camden. His family owned a farm, cotton fields, and a smokehouse in the black part of Camden. Herbert's father, Papa Henry, was a preacher, just like many other Aaron men before him

Herbert wanted to break away. He did not want to be a preacher. He didn't want to farm.

He wanted out of Camden. He wanted to move to the big city. He wanted a new chance.

It was the 1930s. Life was hard all over America, so hard that people called it The Great Depression. It was the time Herbert made up his mind to leave Camden.

Money and jobs were hard to find during the Depression. But a hundred miles down the Alabama River in Mobile there was work repairing ships at the Mobile docks. It was hard, hot work, and it didn't pay much. But it was a start. It was a way out of Wilcox County, and Herbert Aaron took it.

Herbert got a job as a boilermaker's assistant, lifting heavy steel plates that were used to repair ships. He left Camden alone, and planned for his teenage bride, Estella, to join him as soon as she was old enough to leave home.

When Estella finally joined Herbert in Mobile, they had nothing but a will to work and high hopes. They rented an apartment in Down The Bay, a black neighborhood within walking distance of the docks where Herbert worked. It was on the east side of Mobile. The sandy streets were lined with small wooden framed houses laid out in rows. Live Oak trees hung heavy with Spanish moss.

Henry Aaron: Dream Chaser

Herbert and Estella Aaron rented a small housing project apartment at the end of Wilkinson Street.

This was not a street-life kind of neighborhood even though the working people there had more free time than they wanted. Herbert and the other workers were often laid off from work during The Great Depression.

Maids and cooks were the biggest number of black workers in Mobile, but Estella Aaron couldn't spend all of her time cooking and cleaning for other people.

She soon was too busy taking care of children of her own.

Sarah was first. Next came Herbert, Jr. Then, on February 5, 1934, Estella's second son, Henry Louis Aaron was born. He was named for his grandfather, Papa Henry.

Henry was a really big healthy baby. He weighed 12 1/4 pounds when he was born. Mama said his skin lay in fat rolls over his joints. Every time she bathed baby Henry she would have to push up the rolls of fat to wash his wrists and ankles.

He was so big when he was born that when people saw him they'd say, "Oh, he looks just like a little man, doesn't he?" The name stuck and the family started to call him *Man*.

After Henry came Gloria. Then Tommie. Later on, three more children came along.

Estella stayed home and looked after her children at 666 Wilkinson Street. Every once in a while she would clean somebody else's house for two dollars, but she was quick to say, "I never hired a baby-sitter in my life."

In their small apartment, all the children shared beds. And they grew almost all of their food. When Henry was grown up, he remembered, "I've gone many, many weeks with just corn bread, butter beans, and collard greens. Maybe we'd have a piece of pork to season the greens, but we were practically vegetarians before we ever heard of the word."

It was a real treat for the family to eat chicken. Estella cut up the chicken in such a way that all of the children would have a piece of thigh. Later, Henry would say, "My mother could do more with a chicken...than most people can do with five chickens."

"We tried to keep a hog in the backyard to kill every year, and everything else came from the garden. You can believe the Aaron kids didn't have any fat on them.

"But we didn't feel sorry for ourselves because everyone else was in the same boat. Nobody made fun of me for wearing my sister's hand me down clothes, because they were probably wearing their sister's clothes, too."

Early one summer morning when Henry was seven years old, he felt Herbert Junior kicking him in the crowded bed.

Henry scooted to the edge of the bed. Herbert rolled over with him and kept on kicking.

"Stop it, Herbert!" Henry snapped.

"You gotta wake up, Man!" Herbert demanded. "Daddy's taking us to Grandma Sis and Papa Henry's today."

Henry groaned. "I don't want to go!"

"You afraid of a little hard work?" Herbert needled.

"No, I just don't want to leave Mama." Henry was not shy to admit that he was a "mama's boy."

He had to go to Wilcox County anyway. Henry, Sarah, Herbert, and Gloria loaded into Daddy's truck for the long, hot ride.

Grandma Sis met them at the door. She was tall and straight as a ramrod, with deep-set eyes and sharp Indian features—a striking woman. Her mother had been half Indian.

Strong and peaceful, the Aaron kids thought she was the best cook there ever was. As soon as they unloaded from the truck, she set out pork with rice and gravy.

"Boy, sit down and eat," she told Henry.

She didn't have to tell him twice.

While the children were eating, Henry's name-sake, Papa Henry, came in. He and Grandma Sis looked a lot different from each other. While she was tall and thin, Papa Henry was short and stocky. Papa Henry was a preacher on Sunday and a farmer during the week.

"Glad you all are here to help out," Papa Henry said as he washed his hands in the washbowl. "I've just come in from feeding the hogs." Papa Henry raised hogs on the farm for the entire neighborhood. When hog-killing time came, Papa Henry gave meat to all of the neighbors.

Neither Papa Henry nor Grandma Sis had much education, but they had a lot of home-grown sense. They believed in respecting other people.

The children didn't go to their grandparent's house to play. They went to work. And work they did, all day every day doing whatever needed to be done on the farm. Grandma Sis would preserve a lot of food during the summer by cooking it and putting it in jars to eat during the winter. The Aaron children would take a lot of the food home to their mother after they helped with the work.

Young Henry's job was to scrub out the jars so Grandma Sis could preserve the food. He loved thinking about all of the beans, corn, okra, and even some meat that they'd have in the winter. The whole family worked hard every day. Every day except Sunday.

"Everybody go get in the wagon," Papa Henry said every Sunday morning.

All the Aaron children piled in the back of the wagon. Papa Henry guided the horse with Grandma Sis sitting beside him on the buckboard. The children wiggled and squirmed all the way to church.

Once they got to church, the wiggling stopped. Papa Henry stood in the pulpit and preached from his heart. The children were expected to sit and listen.

When he was grown up, Henry Aaron was proud to say, "People in my family say I'm like Papa Henry in a lot of ways– deliberate and good at making decisions. I hope I picked up a few things from him, because he was a wise man."

Before he was eight years old, people noticed that there was something different about Henry Aaron. He loved baseball more than anything else in the world.

At his home on Wilkinson Street, there was no

place to play. No ball diamond. Not even a vacant field. So Henry hit bottle caps with a broom handle under the big water oak in the front yard.

Herbert Sr. realized how crazy his little boy was about baseball. He asked a lady down the street, "Miss Vivian, do you think you could make my little boy a baseball suit?"

Miss Vivian shook her head. "Mmm, Mmm, Mmm," she snorted, "A baseball suit for such a little fellow?" But, make it she did.

Henry loved his baseball suit.

He also loved for his Uncle Bubba Underwood, from Mama's side of the family, to visit. Uncle Bubba was one of the best baseball players in all of Mobile.

Uncle Bubba would come over to the house, sit back and say, "Man, you just comb my hair a hundred times, and after that maybe we can go outside and have ourselves a catch."

Henry eagerly grabbed the comb and set to work. He would gladly do anything to get Uncle Bubba to teach him about baseball.

In 1942, when Henry was eight years old, the Aaron family moved from Down the Bay.

They were going to Toulminville. It was little more than a move across town.

But for Henry, it was like going to Heaven.

In Toulminville there was a vacant field.

A place for baseball.

Not broomstick-and-bottle-cap ball under an oak tree on a crowded street.

Real baseball!

Henry with his parents in Mobile

2

THE CITY LIMITS OF MOBILE ended at Davis Avenue, about a mile from the docks. A little further north, on the other side of Davis Avenue, lay the village of Toulminville.

It was so country that garbage pickup was provided by the pigs that people raised there. Toulminville was known for its oak groves and for a country fair that was put on by Theophilus Toulmin, a relative of the man who the town was named for. By the early 1940s, a few black families began moving there to escape the crowding of Mobile.

The Aaron's move to Toulminville happened one board and one brick at a time.

Henry was eight when his father started bringing home pieces of old lumber and used bricks. Every afternoon after school, Henry was told to chip the mortar off of the old bricks. Herbert Junior had to pull the nails out of the used lumber.

"What do we want with these bricks and lumber, Daddy?" Herbert Junior wanted to know.

"Well, son, the way I look at it, we can move out of Down The Bay," Daddy explained, "And we'll build a house of our own over in Toulminville."

"Herbert, don't be getting any strange ideas," Mama warned. "I don't want to move out to the woods."

"Now, Estella, the way I've got it figured, I can buy four lots over there for a hundred dollars apiece," Daddy said. "Then, the boys and I will build us six rooms, which is twice as many as we are used to. We won't have to pay the nine dollars a month rent any more. Taxes won't be that much. And, it will be a house of our own. I've always wanted something for myself, and we'll have three or four acres of land for the children to play on."

As much as Estella didn't want to leave city life, she realized that the five Aaron children that she already had were crowding the bedroom. So, she agreed with Herbert's plan.

It was not long before the walls and roof were up, and the Aarons were ready to move. The house had no windows; light came from a kerosene lamp. The bathroom was an outhouse in the backyard. The front room was made of the knotty wood from pine trees called lighter knots, because it was good for starting fires. That kind of wood wasn't meant for floors. Every time the floor was scrubbed, splinters rose up from the boards. When the children would run through the house, which was most of the time, long splinters would stick in their bare feet.

"We would hope it didn't rain that hard because it rained more inside than it did outside," Henry later said about his Toulminville home. "But it was our home, and we did the best that we could."

Henry's new address was 2010 Edwards Street. There were only three houses on the street when the house was built. Most of the land was vacant, with a dairy on the corner. There were "country things on every side of us– cows, chickens, hogs, cornfields, sugar cane, watermelon patches, pecan groves, and blackberry thickets," Henry said.

A big ditch ran in the front of the house. On the other side of the ditch was a large field. All of the neighbors pitched in and planted different crops there. One year, the Aarons would grow Irish potatoes. The next year, they would grow sweet potatoes. One neighbor would raise chickens and another neighbor would raise a hog. Then, the neighbors would share their food.

The streets were mushy sand most of the time and cars were always getting stuck.

Yet, Henry remembers, "I enjoyed my childhood. We didn't have anything. When it was seven o'clock, it was dark—and I mean dark. We lived by the light of the kerosene lamp and the water outside."

All of the children had chores. When Daddy came home from work, he wanted a warm bath. "Boys, you need to split up this chore," Daddy said. "Herbert Junior, when I come home on Monday, Wednesday, and Friday, I expect you to have the water pumped, brought in, and warmed for my bath. Man, the rest of the week that job will be yours to do."

Once in a while, Henry and Herbert Junior would get busy playing and forget about their job. Estella had a way of reminding them. She could plait, or braid, switches together to sting their little legs. Estella would pop their legs and the switches would never break, they'd just bend.

Phew! Phew! Phew! Phew! After a few licks, Henry would say, "I don't want this any more. I'll be glad to go and fetch Daddy's water or whatever else you want me to do."

Some might have thought the Aaron house looked poor. But Henry and his family were proud of their new home. The way they looked at it, the only people they knew who owned their own homes were rich folks.

And now they owned one too.

Inside the Toulminville home today is nothing like it was when Henry was growing up there. Today, the sitting room is a trophy room, not only for Henry's many awards, but for all the Aaron brothers and sisters.

3

HERBERT STILL WORKED as a boilermaker's
assistant at the docks. His job was to hold up sixty-
pound steel plates while another worker riveted, or
attached, them to a ship. The job paid eight dollars a
week.

Times were still hard, and Herbert was laid off
almost as often as he was working. But Henry didn't
feel like times were hard. His childhood was filled with
fun.

He made his own toys. One of his favorites was
what he called a roller packer.

Every time Mama emptied a gallon of Alaga Syrup,
she made sure Henry got the empty tin can.

"Oh boy! Come on Cornelius and let's make us a
roller packer," Henry called to his best friend who was
never far away.

Mama chuckled as she went back inside to mop
the floor. That boy sure could entertain himself.

Henry peeled the red and yellow label from the Alaga can. He could smell the rich, dark cane syrup that carried his family through many meals. Cane syrup and Mama's biscuits—a good meal for a poor family.

Henry and Cornelius packed the empty can with dirt from the yard. When they had it full, they mashed the dirt down really tight and put the lid back on the can. Then, they would take a nail and pound on the side of the can until they made a nail hole.

The boys then straightened out a clothes hanger, stuck one end in the nail hole, and bent it. Then, they could roll their roller packer all over the yard. It was their own invention.

One day, Henry found an old bicycle rim that a neighbor had thrown away. Henry didn't have a bicycle, but he had an idea of how to get one.

He saved the old rim.

For a long time he gathered up other old pieces of bicycles that people had thrown away.

He'd save every part so that finally, piece by piece, he put together a bicycle of his own.

After the Aarons had lived in Toulminville for a few years, the city cleared a pecan grove that was on the other side of a vacant lot across the street from their house. The neighborhood kids carved out their own baseball diamond. Then, the city built an "official" diamond on the spot. It became Carver Park, the first recreational park for blacks in all of Mobile.

"It was like having Ebbets Field in my backyard," Henry said. Really, Carver Park was nothing like the real Ebbets Field, the grand, two storied, multi-windowed home of the Brooklyn Dodgers from 1914 until 1957. But it was just as grand to Henry.

"I'd be over there everyday after school and in the summer, usually with my neighbor, Cornelius Giles, and anybody else who could get out of his chores."

When Henry and Cornelius weren't playing baseball at the park, they would play with broomsticks and bottle caps in the yard or the street.

"Those boys are always together," Estella said. "And they are always playing ball."

Late in the afternoons, after it was too dark for ball, Henry and Cornelius sometimes would "cook out."

Henry would gather some vegetables from the garden—potatoes, a turnip, some okra, and a tomato.

Henry would get the old pot that he and Cornelius cooked in, cut up the vegetables and draw some water from the well.

"Cornelius, you got the fire started?" Henry yelled as he came around the corner of the house.

"'Course I do!" Cornelius replied.

"Let's heat up the water and go get the crawfish, then," Henry said.

The boys hurried down to the deep ditch that ran in front of Henry's house. They waded into the murky water. They couldn't see their feet once they had waded into the ditch. They dipped their bare hands down into the unknown darkness, feeling for the crawfish.

"Watch out for those pinchers," they'd remind each other every once in while.

Finally, the boys had enough crawfish for their meal. They hurried back to the pot boiling on the fire, quickly popped off the crawfishs' heads and dropped them into the boiling water along with the vegetables from the garden.

"I sure do wish our pot had a lid," said Cornelius.

"Ain't that the truth," Henry agreed as he ate. "Reckon what kind of bugs got mixed in with our cooking tonight?"

The boys laughed.

"You got a nickel?" Cornelius wanted to know.

"'Course not." Henry replied. "Why?"

"I thought we could go down to the grocery and

get a cookie with some icing inside it," said Cornelius.

"As long as we're wishing for some money, make it a dime, Henry said. "That way, we could get a cookie with some icing on the outside, too."

"You want to sneak over to the neighbor's garden and get a watermelon to bust open?" Cornelius asked.

"Sounds like a good dessert to me!" Henry agreed.

After the boys had eaten all the watermelon they could hold, they went to sit under the streetlight to talk and brag.

"I'm the best pitcher in this town," Cornelius crowed.

"And I can hit better than anybody at Carver Park," Henry exclaimed as he lay back against the sandy curb.

"Other than playing ball and eating, we didn't do a whole lot," Henry later said, "I'd lay on the floor at home and read Dick Tracy comic books for hours at a time. If Cornelius was over, we'd shoot marbles—I was as good as anybody in Toulminville."

Henry was a Boy Scout and proud of it.

Herbert and Estella thought that Boy Scouts would give Henry the chance to be the type of boy that they wanted him to be—the kind of boy who would go out into the woods learning the good nature of life rather than the type of boy who would be out throwing rocks and making trouble. "There was a lot of the Boy Scouts in my mother and especially my father," Henry said later. "They believed in some of the same things that the Boy Scouts believed in. They tried to teach all of us the value and concern for other people in life."

A big event for Henry was the Colored Mardi Gras in Mobile. The Boy Scouts got to direct traffic during the carnival. To be able to direct traffic at Lafayette and Davis Avenue, Henry had to learn all of the Boy Scout laws and do all of the things that he was supposed to do.

The corner of Lafayette and Davis was so valuable because it was a four-way intersection and cars would be coming from all directions. Henry thought, *If I can direct traffic at that intersection, I'll really be somebody, standing up there blowing my whistle and stopping traffic. The world will be at my feet!*

Finally, the day of the Mardi Gras arrived. There was only one problem. It was cold, and Henry only had short Boy Scout pants. Daddy couldn't afford to buy him long pants.

"Henry, it's too cold for you to be out there in those short pants!" his sister Sarah bossed.

"Sarah, I know it's cold out," Henry agreed. "But, I'm not about to give up my post at Davis Avenue and

Lafayette. That is one of the best places to be."

"You're gonna freeze," Sarah warned.

When he got home that afternoon, Sarah asked him how it had gone.

"Everybody was telling me it was cold, but it was warm as the dickens to me!" Henry proudly replied.

Another part of Henry's training in the Boy Scouts was learning how to catch rattlesnakes. He took his handkerchief and wiggled it over the rattlesnake's hole. The rattlesnake came out to grab the handkerchief. Henry quickly snatched the handkerchief and pulled out the rattlesnake's teeth.

Later, when Henry looked back on his childhood, he remembered, "I never knew problems or tensions. It was normal, everyday, average Negro American life."

One night, Henry and his Daddy were sitting out on the back porch when an airplane flew over their house.

"Daddy, I want to be a pilot when I grow up," Henry said.

Daddy replied, "Ain't no colored pilots."

"Okay, then," said Henry. "I'll be a ballplayer."

Daddy shook his head, "Ain't no colored ballplayers, either."

Before long, that was going to change.

4

HENRY DREAMED about being a baseball player.
A baseball player in the big leagues.

But there were things that had to come first. In the
Aaron family, everyone in the family had to pitch in
and help.

One of Henry's first jobs was to pick blackberries
that grew in patches throughout Toulminville.

The sun was hot and the briars scratched his legs
as Henry stooped over each bush, sliding his hand
carefully among the thorns to get the shiny purple-
black berries without getting scratched.

By the time that Henry was through, his back
ached, his bare feet were scraped and sore, his
scratched legs stung, and his fingers were stained with
juice.

Then the selling part began. Henry took his
bucket of blackberries and went door to door.

"Ma'am, would you care to buy some blackberries

today?" Henry would ask. The lady looked over the bucket of berries and told Henry how much she'd pay him. Sometimes, people offered Henry only a quarter for his blackberries. Other times, he might get as much as a dollar.

Herbert found another way for the family to make some extra money. He opened a little tavern next to the house. He named it The Black Cat Inn. Sarah ran the tavern for Daddy. It was the only tavern for black people in Toulminville. It was a lively place with music and dancing and people coming and going.

Daddy ran a little pick-up baseball game out of his tavern. People who came to the tavern could go outside and join in a game. Daddy never played much himself because he was more concerned with trying to make money from the refreshments that he sold. Daddy took an icebox and put chipped ice in it. He filled the icebox with drinks, and as the game went on Henry was supposed to sell the drinks to the players and spectators.

"Henry, stand up in the back of the truck," Daddy said. "See if you can sell enough cold drinks so we can buy a pound of bologna today."

"Daddy, please let me play with the team today," Henry begged.

"When you sell all of these sodas, you can come and play baseball," Daddy promised.

"That's how I got to play baseball on his team. Hurry up and sell those sodas," Henry said later. "Now, I don't know if I got rid of some of them or not. But, I wanted to play baseball."

As Henry got older, he went to work for two brick masons. That was hard work for a young boy. Henry carried loads of bricks from one place to another. He didn't complain because he knew Mama and Sarah were at home waiting to see how much money they could add to the family's pot.

"I carried my money home to my mother because we needed it," Henry said. "And we did the very best that we could."

Henry worked jobs in the summer, too. He mowed lawns and picked potatoes. The potato truck would come by at seven each morning. He would hop on and the driver would take him out in the country to the potato fields. Henry would return home around suppertime with eight or nine dollars in his pocket.

Henry's favorite job, though, was delivering ice. The ice came in twenty-five pound blocks, and he had tongs to carry it into people's houses.

Later on, Henry told sportswriters that he built up

his wrists by hauling ice up flights of stairs. He was joking when he said that. "The truth is, I didn't have that job for very long," Henry admitted. "My mistake was that I told them I'd drive the truck, although I was only 14 and didn't quite know how to drive yet. I was doing all right until I pulled away from a stop when I was on a hill and all of the ice went sliding off the back of the truck."

All of the Aaron children had chores, and Mama expected them to get their work done before they went off to play.

Henry was always in a hurry to finish so that he could join the other boys playing baseball at Carver Park.

One day, he and Herbert Junior were cutting wood for the stove.

"Henry, I saw you sneak some of your sticks from my pile!" Herbert Junior complained.

"I've got to get through here so I can go and play ball," Henry explained. "The game started without me."

"You know how Mama feels about us getting our work done," his brother reminded him.

"Oooh, don't I ever!" Henry replied as he thought about Mama's switchings. "I sure don't want her whaling on us today."

Henry finished picking up his stack of wood.

Meanwhile, the game had started without him. After a couple of innings, some of the boys asked a boy named Robert Driscoll when Henry was coming.

"You know he's late most of the time because his Mama has him doing chores," Robert said. "I just hope he gets here before we're up to bat again."

A few minutes later, the boys saw Henry's head bobbing up and down through the cornfield. He had a path beaten through the field with vines growing up on either side.

"Put the bat down, Robert," Henry yelled. "I'm going to pinch hit."

The boys always let him bat when he got to the game.

They didn't mind that Henry's way of batting looked odd. Henry was right handed. Almost all right handed batters hold the bat with their right hand above their left hand. But Henry held the bat with his left hand on top. Ball players call that "cross-handed."

If it had been anyone other than Henry, the other players might have made fun of him. But none of them did, because even batting cross handed, Henry was the best batter in the park!

Henry continued working to help out the family

and playing ball whenever there was free time. The
ball playing was his passion. He thought about it
during the day and when he lay down at night, visions
of hitting baseballs came to him in dreams.

They were dreams that would not go away, no
matter how much he was told to forget them.

Mama was especially concerned about his fascina-
tion with baseball. "It's not that I have anything against
the game, son, or against you playing it," Mama said.
"But it bothers me that you are more interested in
baseball than anything else, including schoolwork. I
have my heart set on you going to college, and baseball could get in the way."

Henry never wanted to do anything that would
displease his mother. So he promised to try harder on
his schoolwork and get all of his chores done. *I really
will try to quit chasing this baseball dream*, he thought
to himself.

He couldn't.

And in the spring of 1947, when Henry Aaron was
fourteen years old, something happened to make his
baseball dreams burn brighter than ever before.

5

IN 1947, BRANCH RICKEY was president of the Brooklyn Dodgers, one of America's most important major league baseball teams.

On April 10, of that year, just five days before the baseball season was to begin, Rickey made a startling announcement.

He told the world that the Dodgers had a new first baseman named Jackie Robinson. It was no big deal that the team had a new first baseman. Baseball teams often hired new players. What made this announcement surprising was that Jackie Robinson was a black man.

No black man had ever before played in major league baseball.

Many white people did not think black men should be allowed to play major league baseball and many of them protested against Robinson.

But it was different in black communities all over

America. Many black people felt that it was a hint, a tiny little hint, that life for black people in America was beginning to change for the better.

Jackie Robinson became the hero of Davis Avenue in Mobile.

When announcer Gordon McLendon broadcast the Dodgers games, everybody got together and crowded around the radio.

Then one day Henry heard news that turned the air electric. Jackie Robinson and the Dodgers were coming to Mobile for an exhibition games with the Mobile Bears. Even better, Robinson was coming a day early to speak at a grocery store on Davis Avenue.

Henry knew he had to be there.

That afternoon Henry played hooky from school and raced to Davis Avenue. He wasn't going to tell Mama and Daddy that he'd missed school to do that!

Henry listened to every word his hero had to say. He listened as closely as he had ever listened to Papa Henry preach. "Never allow yourself to be satisfied with the way things are," Robinson told his black audience.

He also said some of the same things that Henry's mother and father often said: "Playing sports is good— it's great! But the most important thing is your education. Stay in school and try to get your education. And, if you decide and you play sports, well, that's just a bonus. Just make sure that you get an education."

Henry left the grocery store with a head full of ideas. Not all of them were about education. Jackie Robinson had breathed baseball into the black community. Henry went straight home to see his Daddy.

"Daddy, I'm gonna be in the big leagues before Jackie Robinson retires!" Henry announced.

Herbert Aaron didn't argue with Henry this time. Daddy seemed to understand that Henry had to play baseball. Mama was the one who still had a hard time accepting it.

"Henry, if you want to play sports so much, why don't you play football?" Mama asked Henry. "You might get a scholarship to college that way."

"That's just it, Mama," Henry replied. "If I got a football scholarship, it would keep me out of baseball."

Mama just shook her head.

So, no one was more surprised than Mama when Henry signed up for football during his sophomore year of high school.

Little did she know that Henry was trying out for football to impress a cute majorette named Queeneta

Jones. *That's where the girls are always looking—at those football players!* Henry thought. *I'd best get over there and start playing football.*

But Henry realized that as much as he loved to watch football, he wasn't impressed with going and slinging his body out there on the field. After a few days, he quit.

Dr. Benjamin Baker, principal of Central High School, didn't want Henry to quit. Henry tried to explain that he didn't want to ruin his chances for a baseball career by playing football. Dr. Baker didn't want to hear that.

The following spring was when Dr. Baker embarrassed Henry and hit him with a cane in front of the whole school.

It was the time that Daddy decided to move Henry from Central High to Josephine Allen Institute, a private school.

But it was spring, and Henry would not have to go to Josephine Allen until fall.

A whole summer of playing ball lay before him.

6

ED SCOTT WAS A PLAYER for the Mobile Black Bears, a semi-professional baseball team. He also was the team manager.

Sometimes when the Black Bears were not playing, Scott would wander over to Toulminville and watch the recreation league games at the park near Henry's house.

Scott kept noticing a young, skinny boy who seemed to always play a little better than all the rest. Who is that boy? Scott wanted to know.

Why, everybody in the neighborhood knows him, was the reply. That's Henry Aaron.

Scott wanted Henry to play for the Black Bears, and Henry wanted to play for them. But Mama would not let him. Her Henry was still just a boy, and the Black Bears' players were mostly grown men. Worst of all, in Mama's opinion, the team played on Sunday, the Lord's day.

Mama told Scott that she would not let Henry play for the Black Bears, but Scott did not take no for an answer. He kept coming and asking.

Scott came so often that Henry hid when he saw him coming.

Henry wasn't sure what wore Mama down, but finally she gave in. She told him he couldn't travel with the Black Bears when they went out of town, but when they were at home in Prichard—just up the road from Toulminville—he could play.

Scott could not believe his eyes when he saw Henry Aaron walking through the gate at Mitchell Field. Henry hurried over to Scott. "If I play for you, do I get a uniform?"

Ed quickly got him a uniform, and Henry played for the rest of the day. He was the Black Bears short-stop every Sunday that they played in town.

The owner of the team, Ed Tucker, paid the players ten dollars after every game. But, he would never pay Henry on Sunday. "Come by my house on Monday to get your money," Tucker would always say.

So, every Monday, Henry would go by Tucker's house to get his money, and Mr. or Mrs. Tucker would always stick a couple of extra dollars in his hand. Henry thought, This is as good as it can get—to be paid to play for the Black Bears.

What Henry did not know was that the Indianapolis Clowns of the Negro American League paid Ed Scott to watch for players who might be good enough for that team. Scott gave Bunny Downs, manager of the Clowns, some reports on Henry. Then he arranged for the Clowns to come to Mitchell Field to play the Black Bears, so Downs could see Henry for himself.

After the game, Downs came up to Henry. "How would you like to play shortstop for the Clowns?" he asked.

Henry knew that there was no way Mama would let him do that. He had to go back to school in the fall, and he told Downs so.

"Well, I'm going to send you a contract anyway," Downs said.

The fact that the Clowns were willing to offer a contract may have thrilled Henry, but the prospect of telling his parents about it was another matter.

He didn't tell them about Downs' offer. He kept it a secret.

Besides, Henry thought that he'd never hear from Bunny Downs again.

Late that summer, the Brooklyn Dodgers held a tryout camp in Mobile for black players. Henry thought, *Wow! To be on the team with Jackie Robinson, Roy Campanella, and Don Newcombe. I always knew that I could join Jackie Robinson someday. This is my chance!*

There was only one problem. The boys from Down the Bay were cocky and knew how to call attention to themselves. Henry was just a quiet, skinny kid who batted cross-handed. When it was his turn to bat, he took a swing or two and some big kid from Down the Bay rushed him out of the box. The scout told Henry that he was too small to play for the Dodgers. *Well, that's that*, Henry thought as he slowly walked home.

Henry felt sad. Ball season was over and he was just a teenager having a hard time with high school.

He went to Josephine Allen and tried his best. But once January arrived, Henry starting checking the mailbox every day to see if the Clowns were going to send for him.

As days passed, the trip to the mailbox got longer and longer. Every day Henry looked for an envelope from the Clowns. Nothing. Nothing.

January turned to February, and spring was about to turn Mobile's azaleas into a rainbow of colors.

But it was a sad, gray time for Henry. His hopes were dashed. He thought no letter was coming.

Then, one day, there it was.

An envelope. *The* envelope.

From the Indianapolis Clowns!

It said that the Clowns would pay Henry $200 a month, and that he was to meet the team for spring training in Winston-Salem, North Carolina.

Henry didn't know what to do. The school term was not over, but he knew he couldn't miss this chance. If he waited around for a white scout to sign him, he might never get a chance to play.

Henry tried to reason with Mama. "I probably won't make the team anyway, Mama. I'll be back in a week or two to finish school."

"But, what if you do make it?" Mama wanted to know.

"I'll still finish school in the off-season if I do make it," Henry promised. "If I don't make it I'll go on to college. Please, Mama."

Estella didn't want Henry to go. But, $200 a month was a lot of money for the Aarons. She knew she had to let him go.

On the day Henry left Mobile to go play for the Clowns, Mama was so upset that she couldn't go to the train station to see him off.

Henry stood in the kitchen watching as she silently made him sandwiches to take on the trip.

"I'll be fine, Mama," Henry said with more confidence than he felt.

Mama stuffed two dollars in his pocket, then stood in the yard crying as Henry rode off with Daddy, Herbert Junior, Sarah, and Ed Scott.

When the group arrived at the train station, Scott handed Henry an envelope.

"Henry, I want you to give this to Bunny Downs when you get to Winston-Salem, North Carolina for camp. Make sure it is unopened," Scott commanded.

Henry's knees banged together as he boarded the train. He had never ridden in anything bigger than a bus or faster than his Daddy's old pickup truck.

The train pulled from the station, slowly at first, then picking up speed. Henry looked back, watching Daddy, Sarah, Herbert Junior, and Mr. Scott get smaller and smaller in the distance.

Henry had never felt so alone in his whole life.

Here he was, barely seventeen years old; a raggedy boy who wore his sister's hand-me-down pants and had never in his life been out of the black part of Mobile, Alabama, except to visit kinfolks in Camden.

He just sat there on the train, clutching his two sandwiches, speaking to no one. He stared out the window at the blur of lonesome pineywoods rushing by, interrupted once in a while by small towns he'd never heard of. He was afraid.

Henry didn't know where he was allowed to go on the train and where black people weren't supposed to go. He walked up and down the aisle a few times and tried to talk himself out of getting off at the next stop and going back home.

One thought kept Henry from getting off. "I knew that I loved to play baseball," he said. "And I had a feeling I might be pretty good at it."

7

NEGRO LEAGUE BASEBALL started a few years after the Civil War, when two black ballclubs, the Brooklyn Uniques and the Philadelphia Excelsiors, played on a crisp October afternoon in Brooklyn, New York.

By the early 1950s, the Negro Leagues were famous, and had been for more than thirty years. Some of the most famous black players were Satchel Paige, Don Newcombe, and Roy Campanella.

After Jackie Robinson was allowed to play for the Dodgers, other black players were picked by white teams, including Paige, Newcombe and Campanella.

By 1952, when Henry joined the Indianapolis Clowns, there were sixteen teams in the major leagues. Only six of them had any black players. But everyone knew that in just a few years the major league teams would hire all the best black players from the Negro Leagues. When that happened, there wouldn't be

Negro Leagues any more.

But in 1952, the Indianapolis Clowns still was a serious Negro League baseball team. In fact, it was the best team in the league.

As more and more black players moved to the major leagues, it became harder and harder for the Negro League to get fans to come to the ballpark and watch the teams play.

The players would have to do special things to get fans to come. Sometimes it would be something funny, like the Harlem Globetrotters do with basketball. In fact, Goose Tatum, one of the famous Globetrotters, had been a first baseman for the Clowns. It was said that Tatum was one of the fanciest first basemen anyone ever saw.

When Henry started with the team, the players were performing a "shadowball" routine during their warm-ups, taking infield practice without a baseball. Then, after the warm-ups, the players turned the clowning over to two clowns named King Tut and Spec Bebop. Tut would pretend to have a toothache and Bebop would yank it out with pliers, or they would pretend to be fishing when the boat turned over. They threw buckets of confetti into the crowd— anything to keep the crowds entertained and coming to the games.

In Winston-Salem, Henry somehow found his way off the train and to the Clown's practice field.

He reported to Bunny Downs and handed him the unopened envelope, just as Scott had directed.

When Scott tore open the envelope, he found a note from Scott. It was only two sentences. "Forget everything else about this player. Just watch his bat!"

Downs did not tell Henry what the note said, not right then.

It was a tough time for the older Clown players. They saw the major league teams hiring away the most talented young black players. They knew they were too old to get chosen and would have to finish their playing days in the Negro league.

Sometimes they would take out their frustration by treating the new players poorly.

They treated Henry like he was a nuisance. They didn't bother to find out if he could hit or not.

Henry began to feel like it was the Dodgers tryout all over again. Every time he would try to step into the batting cage, some older player would charge in and tell him to get out of the way.

Henry would move to the sidelines, shivering in the threadbare shirt he wore for practice. The older players had jackets, but they would not give one to a teenage rookie.

Henry may not have even made the team, except for an accident.

One of the regular infielders got hurt.

The Clowns needed a replacement. And quick.

Henry might not have been who they wanted.

But he was the one who was available at that moment.

At 17-years-old, Henry Aaron was in the starting lineup for the Indianapolis Clowns.

As scared as I am about everything else, I know that I can hit a baseball, he thought.

He knew himself well. As soon as he started batting, the hits started coming!

Pretty soon, the fans started talking about what a good hitter the new young shortstop was.

It was an exciting time. Henry was getting lots of chances to play.

Still, it was a tough time for black ball players.

On trips to play teams in other towns, the Clowns seldom stopped in a restaurant because it was hard to find one that would serve black people. The players would just buy groceries when they saw a store and eat on the highway.

Once, the team was to play a doubleheader at Griffith Stadium in Washington, D.C. The game was delayed by rain so the players decided to eat while they waited for the rain to stop. They went into a restaurant and ordered their food.

After they had eaten and were about to leave the restaurant, the players heard dishes being smashed to pieces in the kitchen. "What a horrible sound," Henry said later. "...They had to destroy the plates that had touched the forks that had been in the mouths of black men. If dogs had eaten off those plates, they'd have washed them."

Henry felt humiliated. His face felt as if it were on fire. He knew this was no more of an insult than having to go to the back in some restaurants to get served or to have to sit on the bus and eat.

He and some of his teammates had a little trick to get food. Sam Jones, a pitcher, was a fair skinned black man. When people looked at him, they were never sure if he was black or white. When the bus arrived in a new town, Henry and the other players would write down their orders on a piece of paper.

Sam would then take the piece of paper, walk down the road a little ways and catch a cab. Nobody stopped him from getting in the cab because they didn't realize he was a black man. Sam went to a white restaurant. When he got inside, he put the piece of paper on the counter to place his order, but never said a word.

"What do you want? How many sandwiches do you want?" the man behind the counter would ask.

Sam shook his head and pointed his finger toward his wide-open mouth, so that the person would think that he couldn't talk. Sam was sure that if he spoke, the man would realize that he was black.

Thinking that Sam couldn't talk, the man quickly started to fill his order. Once Sam had all of the sandwiches, he caught a cab back out to the bus and brought the other players their meal.

Henry wanted things to change, and he remembered the words of Jackie Robinson that he had heard back on Davis Avenue: "You should never allow yourself to be satisfied with the way things are." Henry didn't know what he could do to make that change. He didn't have an answer and nobody could give him an answer. *All I want to do is eat and play baseball*, Henry thought. Henry learned that to survive he would just have to do whatever was necessary when he was dealing with white people.

"You just made do with what you had to do and did it the best that you could," Henry later recalled.

Henry did not know it at the time, but his ability to hit the ball so well made him valuable to the owner of the Clowns, Syd Pollock, in a special sort of way.

Since Negro League baseball was not as popular as it once was, the owners of the teams always were looking for ways to make enough money to pay the bills. One way was to sell good young players to major league teams.

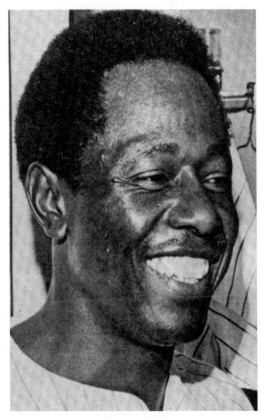

What Henry did not know at the time was that Pollock was offering him to the big leagues. Pollock wrote a letter to John Mullen, of the Boston Braves. Pollock's letter was not about Henry in particular, but at the bottom he added a note: "P.S. We've got

A happy Henry Aaron in his playing days

an 18-year-old shortstop batting cleanup for us." That was Henry.

Then, the New York Giants started to hear about Henry, too. Pretty soon, scouts from other teams started coming to Clowns games to watch Henry play. Several of them told him they wanted him on their team, including the Braves. He knew that he would have to make a decision soon, but he didn't know what to do.

"I am having a good time," Henry told his family. "The other players are even talking to me now. Besides, none of the scouts are saying anything about giving me any money to sign for them."

A few nights later, when the team was playing in Oklahoma, Henry received a phone call. It was Ed Scott and he was at Mama and Daddy's house. "Henry, if the opportunity comes up to sign with a big-league team, you have to take it," he said. "You just can't pass it up."

After the phone call, Henry talked to Pollock, the Clown's owner. "Mr. Pollock, I will go to the Braves if you think that is what I should do," Henry said.

Pollock picked up the phone and called John Mullen of the Braves. They made a deal over the telephone that gave them the exclusive right for thirty days to offer Henry a position on the Braves. If they did not make the offer within 30 days, he could remain on the Clowns or another team could make an offer.

Days passed and Henry did not hear from the Braves, even though the newspapers were writing wonderful stories about him. The *Chicago Defender* reported: "Major league scouts are swarming to parks where the Clowns are playing to get a good look at the young Aaron...All seem to agree that he stands at the plate like a Ted Williams."

During a game in Buffalo, New York, Henry noticed a man standing by a rail. Henry knew the man was a scout. The man came over to Henry.

"I am Dewey Griggs of the Braves," the man said. "I am a little concerned about your style of playing. You field the ball on one knee and then throw it underhanded to first base. Can you really throw?"

Before Henry could answer, Griggs continued, "You ease around the field at about three-quarters speed most of the time. Can you run?"

"Why, yes sir, I can," Henry replied. "My Daddy told me never to hurry unless I had to, but if you want to see me run and throw, I'll do what I can."

"One other thing, Henry," said Griggs. "Why don't you hold your bat with your right hand on top instead of cross-handed?"

The next time Henry came to bat he held the bat the right way and hit a home run. The time after that, he bunted and raced to first base to show Griggs that he could run. Whenever a ball was hit to him in the field, he made sure that he threw it overhand to first base as hard as he could.

Griggs was satisfied.

That night, Griggs wrote a letter to John Mullen.

May 25, 1952

Dear John:

Scouted the double header between Indianapolis and Memphis at Buffalo Sunday afternoon. Heavy showers in the morning left the playing field in a muddy condition and prevented good fielding.

Henry Aaron the seventeen year old shortstop of the Indianapolis Club looked very good...On June 15th Indianapolis plays two games with Kansas City at Buffalo and at that time I will give you a complete story on the boy. I am satisfied with the boy's hitting. However, I want to see him make plays both to his right and left and slow hit balls that he has to come in after. Also another look at his throwing. This boy could be the answer.

Sincerely yours,

Dewey S. Griggs

When John Mullen received the letter, his thirty-days of exclusive rights to hire Henry were over.

On May 29, Pollock received telegrams from both the Braves and the Giants with offers to hire Henry. Henry looked at the offers carefully. "I thought my chances to make the Braves were better and that they were being fairer to me, paying me more money to play in a lower classification," Henry said. When the time came for Henry to sign his contract with the Braves, his signature wasn't enough to make the contract legal. He was still too young. To make the contract legal, his Daddy had to sign too.

When the time came for Henry to report to the Braves, Pollock gave him a cardboard suitcase for the trip. His first assignment was not actually to play for the Braves. The Braves had several teams playing in smaller towns where they assigned new players to improve their skills. These smaller town teams are called the "farm" teams of the major league team.

On June 8, 1952, Henry Aaron boarded his first airplane, bound for fame and fortune at the Braves' farm team in Eau Claire, Wisconsin.

"I was a nervous wreck," said Henry, "bouncing around in the sky over part of the country I'd hardly ever heard about, much less been to, headed for a white town to play ball with white boys."

8

EAU CLAIRE, WISCONSIN in 1952 wasn't a bad place for a black person, except that Henry was just about the only black person there.

Every day Henry left the YMCA, where he was staying, to walk to the ball field, Carson Park. On his way he passed the only other black man in the town who was not a baseball player, a guy who stood on a corner flipping a silver dollar.

Henry felt odd, being one of only a handful of black men around all those white people.

"You know I'm not much of a talker anyway," he told his family, "But, here you can't pry my mouth open. My way of talking is not like the way people talk in Wisconsin. I probably won't say more than fifty words this whole summer unless I'm talking to Wes (Covington) or Julie (Bowers), the only other black players on the club."

"I stayed there for two months, and I doubt I was

out in the town for two hours the whole time," Henry later recalled.

Henry spent most of his free time listening to the Chicago Cubs and the White Sox on the radio.

"There was a park with a nice lake right outside the stadium, and on game days Hank and some of the guys would bring fishing poles and just sit out there fishing until it was time to get in uniform," recalled Henry's teammate Wes Covington. "It didn't take much to keep him happy. Hank could get total relaxation out of things that other people would find boring."

Talking in front of the white people didn't worry Henry nearly as much as something else. He was worried about the idea of playing ball against white boys. *I wonder if those guys have something I've never seen before*, Henry thought.

It didn't take long for Henry to realize "the ball was still round after it left a white pitcher's hand, and it responded the same way when you hit it with a bat."

In his first game, Henry batted seventh out of the nine batters. He came up to bat for the first time in the second inning, and was more nervous than he had ever been. It was his first time to bat against a white pitcher. As soon as Henry smashed a hard single over third base, and he instantly knew that everything would be fine.

The next day, *The Eau Claire Leader* published the first newspaper story ever written about Henry Aaron as a member of a major league baseball organization.

It was an article that first called him by the name that most people know him today—Hank:

Hank Aaron, 18-year-old Negro League short-stop, made an auspicious beginning by banging out singles in his first two trips, driving home Collins Morgan, who had hit doubles to deep center field each time. Aaron handled seven chances but muffed a potential double play ball as St. Cloud scored the deciding runs in the sixth inning.

Henry batted second after his first night of baseball. He didn't hit a home run until his second week. The home run came at the right time for Henry because he was thinking about quitting.

He was lonesome in Wisconsin.

He was having trouble on the field too.

During one game while Henry was playing short stop, a ground ball was hit to the second baseman. There was a runner on first base, so the second baseman flipped the ball to Henry to get that runner out. Then Henry was supposed to throw to first base to get out the runner who had just hit the ball. It would be a double play—two outs from one batter.

Henry caught the toss from the second baseman, but when he threw toward first, it smacked the runner coming toward second square in the forehead. The runner had to be carried off the field on a stretcher and wasn't able to play baseball again. Henry felt terrible.

Another time, Henry decided to take batting practice left handed, hoping to learn to bat both left handed and right handed. A player who can do that is called a switch-hitter, and is more valuable to a team than a player who can just hit one way.

Henry stepped into the batting cage, a screened area where players practiced batting.

"Unlike today, the batting cages weren't the most protective things in the world," Henry remembers. "These cages had big holes in them."

As Henry was fooling around waiting to hit, the bat slipped loose from his hand. It flew through the air and smacked Julie Bowers in the face. Henry had broken his teammate's nose!

Henry called his Daddy in Mobile. "I'm feeling so awful about all these things that I'm ready to pack up my cardboard suitcase. I'm coming home, Daddy," Henry declared. "I'm so homesick."

Herbert Junior was right by the phone, listening to his Daddy's side of the conversation. When Herbert Junior realized how the conversation was going, he took the phone. "Henry, you'd be crazy to leave. There is nothing in Mobile that is going to be any better than where you are. If you leave you'll be walking out on the best break you could ever hope to get."

Henry hung up and started thinking about what Herbert Junior had said. *He's right. If I give up baseball now, I'll never have the opportunity to meet as many people, or go as many places, or be as involved in as many things. I don't think I can be as successful in anything else.*

Henry felt better after that. Within a few weeks, he was the best hitter in the league.

In July, Henry was selected to play in the Northern League All-Star Game, and at the end of the season, Henry was named Rookie of the Year for the Northern League.

After the season was over, Henry didn't go right back to Mobile. Instead, he rejoined the Indianapolis Clowns to travel the country playing exhibition games during the fall. The Clowns and the Birmingham Black Barons played a 13-game series throughout the South.

Henry Aaron: Dream Chaser

It was a special series for Henry because some of the games were going to be in Mobile, his home town. He hadn't been home since he'd left in the spring. Henry was given a big welcome and the Dragon Social Club, a black organization, honored him by calling it Henry Aaron Day at Hartwell Field. Henry thought this was strange since he'd never before played a game at that field, and now they were naming the day for him.

The series ended in New Orleans, and when it did, Henry headed straight home to Mobile, two hours away.

He could hardly wait to hear what Daddy and Mama would say about his season.

"Son, I've been bragging on you to everybody," Daddy said as soon as Henry got home. "You should be mighty proud."

"Thank you, Daddy," Henry replied. "Mama, now do you feel better about me playing baseball than when I left?"

Mama admitted that she did. "But," Mama added, "You still have to go back to Josephine Allen and get your degree."

Henry knew there was no getting around it.

"No matter what I do on the ball field," Henry realized, "Mama isn't going to cut me loose until I graduate from high school."

So, the baseball star became a school boy again.

9

IN 1953, there were no major league baseball teams further South than St. Louis, Missouri and Cincinnati, Ohio.

This meant that while Jackie Robinson was the first black professional baseball player in all of the United States, he only had to play in the North.

In those days, the South had many minor-league farm teams. For black players on those southern farm teams for the first time, it was a scary and, sometimes, dangerous experience.

It was a land of ugly stories. In towns like Birmingham and Montgomery, it was against the law for blacks and whites to even play checkers or dominoes together. How much harder was it going to be for them to play on the same baseball teams?

The South Atlantic League—called the Sally League—had teams in Montgomery, Alabama; Columbus, Augusta, and Savannah, Georgia; Columbia and

Charleston, South Carolina; and Jacksonville, Florida.

It was into this unknown and frightening territory that the Milwaukee Braves sent three promising young black players—Henry Aaron, Horace Garner, and Felix Mantilla.

At the end of training camp in Waycross, Georgia, a manager called out the farm team assignments for each player. "Henry Aaron, Bus 5, you're going to Jacksonville. Felix Mantilla, Bus 5. Horace Garner, Bus 5. Pack your things and be on the bus tomorrow morning. You've got to get to Jacksonville to be ready to play the Red Sox in a practice game."

Then the coach pulled them to the side, with big and scary news. "The three of you will be breaking the color line in the Sally League." It meant that they would be the first black men ever to play on major league farm teams in the South.

Henry was more nervous about that than about his new assignment.

The game against the Red Sox was called a "historic event" by the *Florida Times-Union* newspaper because the black men were going to play.

As soon as Henry took the field, he heard boos. Then some fans called him ugly names. Henry put the fans out of his mind when the Red Sox began to beat

Jacksonville. The Red Sox whipped Jacksonville 14-1.

Henry called home to report his first game to his family. "I could take some satisfaction in the fact that our one home run was the one I hit in the eighth inning." Henry hoped his team would do better in the regular season.

There were a few free days before the season started. Henry, Felix, and Horace used the time to find a place to live. There was a black man named Manuel Rivera who had a house near the ballpark. He agreed

Young Henry as a minor league player for Jacksonville, Florida

to let them move in.

A day or two later, Henry was hanging around the ballpark when he noticed a girl going into the nearby post office. He called over T.C. Marlin, the clubhouse manager, who knew everybody in Durkeeville, the black part of Jacksonville.

"T.C., who is that girl?" Henry asked.

"That's Barbara Lucas," T.C. said. "She's just come home from Florida A&M to attend classes here at the business college."

"Will you call her over here and introduce me to her?" he asked. "Be sure and tell her that I am one of the next great stars of baseball."

T.C. called Barbara over. Henry smiled and shook her hand as T.C. introduced them. He didn't think she was very impressed with what T.C. said about his baseball skills, but he asked her for a date anyway.

"You'll have to come home and meet my parents before I can think about going out with you," Barbara said.

"O.K. then, where do you live?" Henry asked.

Barbara motioned to the housing project across from the park. Henry went to meet her parents. For the rest of the summer, whenever the team played in town, Henry would spend his free time on Barbara's front porch eating her mother's coconut cake.

The team won the first official game of the season in Savannah, Georgia. They continued to win—seven games in a row before they lost one. The Jacksonville paper wrote that they might be one of the best Class A teams ever put together.

The Sally League had counted on Henry, Felix, and Horace to do well in Jacksonville, so that they could make it easier for more black players to be assigned to southern teams. The league also expected them to keep their cool and not fight back against white players or fans who were calling them names or being mean to them in other ways. When pitchers threw at them, they had to get up and swing at the next pitch. When somebody called them names, they had to pretend they didn't hear.

Some people threatened to kill the black players. Joe Andrews, a white first baseman, became the black players' buddy. When the black players left the ballpark after a game, he carried a bat with him and told them to stick close to his side.

During one game, the pitcher kept throwing the ball at Henry's head. White players on the other team and the fans were calling Henry names. Joe could tell that Henry was getting upset.

"What's wrong, Henry?" he asked.

Henry just shook his head and said, "I don't want to hurt nobody. I just want to play baseball."

Henry was only nineteen years old. Having to be an example for black players to follow was hard to do.

By the end of his first season in the Sally League, Henry Aaron had the highest batting average and had batted in more runs than any other player. He also had another record. This one he did not want. He made thirty-six errors at second base. "I was a butcher at second base," he said. "Felix used to say a guy could get killed trying to run double plays with me." Henry laughed and added, "We all knew that my best position was some other position."

The Sally League was divided in two divisions. The Jacksonville team ended the season in first place in their division. Because of that, they got to go to a playoff against the team from Columbia, South Carolina, which was first in its division.

Jacksonville lost in the playoffs.

Henry was disappointed to lose, but he knew something good had happened that summer. He, Felix, and Horace had played baseball in the South. As Henry put it:

We had played a season of great baseball in the

Deep South, under circumstances that nobody had experienced before—and because of us, never would again. We had shown the people of Georgia and Alabama and South Carolina and Florida that we were good ball players and decent human beings, and that all it took to get along together was to get a little more used to each other.

After the playoffs, the only thing left was a banquet for the team in Jacksonville. Henry received the award for the league's Most Valuable Player.

After the ceremony, Henry walked over to the telephone and called Barbara to ask her to marry him.

"You'll have to ask my Daddy," Barbara replied.

"Well, put him on the phone, then," Henry laughed.

Mr. Lucas agreed even though he was worried that a black player might not have much of a chance to make a decent living in baseball.

On October 6, 1953, Henry and Barbara married.

Not long afterward, another big chance came up. Felix was going to Puerto Rico to play winter baseball, and he wanted Henry and Barbara to come along.

Henry thought it was a great idea—"a little money and all the ballplaying I could get."

10

CAGUAS IS AN INLAND CITY on the Caribbean island of Puerto Rico, just a few miles south of the capital city of San Juan.

It was not the island's largest city, but it had a good baseball team.

It was the team that Henry played on.

Henry loved playing baseball in Caguas. But, it didn't start off that way. He was fielding poorly, and his hitting average was low. The team managers were ready to send Henry back to Mobile, but Felix talked them into letting him stay.

"That turned out to be one of the best things anybody ever did for me," said Henry. "If I had gone back to Mobile, I almost surely would have been drafted into the army."

Henry was playing so badly that something had to be done. Team manager Mickey Owen talked to him.

"Henry, how about trying the outfield?" Owen

said.

"Okay. I'm probably going to be drafted into the army anyway," Henry answered. "I'll do whatever you want until the draft board calls."

Owen sent Henry into the field and hit him some fly balls. Henry turned, ran, and caught them.

"Well, Henry, you sure can catch the ball," Owen said. "But, can you throw it?

"Let's try it and see," Henry suggested.

Owen hit Henry some ground balls and told him to charge them and throw to second base. Henry threw the ball overhand right to second base.

"Now, Henry," Owen instructed. "Really cut loose and throw one to third."

Henry threw the ball hard. It came across the infield as well as any one else's throws. That was it! Henry Aaron was an outfielder.

Henry was delighted, as it turned out. His hitting picked up. He got to bat against major league pitching almost every day. When it came time for the All-Star game, Henry was hitting well enough to be picked. It would be his third All-Star game at three different positions in three different leagues in two years.

Henry and Barbara's first child, Gaile, was born in Puerto Rico and spent her first couple of months in the little house they rented there.

"Caguas was kind of a country town," Henry remembered. "One of my lasting memories of Puerto Rico is hearing a bell ringing in our backyard and looking out to find a cow eating Gaile's diapers off the clothesline."

Henry and Barbara got back to Mobile in time to spend a few weeks before spring training began. Henry was delighted to hear that he would be in Bradenton, Florida, trying out for the major league team. He wanted to play in Milwaukee when the regular season began. But, he thought, *That dream is still a long way off.*

What Henry could not predict was that Bobby Thompson, the Braves' left fielder, would break his ankle while playing a spring practice game in St. Petersburg, Florida.

The coach replaced Thompson with Henry.

Henry played as hard as he could. He thought, *I'm playing in an organization that will give me every opportunity to be with the team and do the best that I can do.* When the team left Bradenton, Florida, Henry had a major-league contract.

America was introduced to Henry Aaron in 1954. One of the stories in the *Milwaukee Sentinel* said, "not since Mickey Mantle was moved up to the Yankees has there been a player with as big a buildup as Aaron, a lithe 19-year-old Negro."

First of all, Henry was already 20-years-old. He laughed to see that the reporter had called him "lithe" or thin. "At that time, I was very skinny," he said. "I couldn't find a pair of pants to fit me. I'm six feet tall and I only weighed 169 or 170 pounds. Maybe it was from all those years of being a vegetarian.

"I also remember the name over my locker being spelled 'Arron,'" Henry said. "And so I don't remember feeling like a phenom in the spring of 1954. Instead I remember telling Barbara to keep the suitcases ready because I didn't expect to be in the big club for long."

The Braves opening game was scheduled in Cincinnati, Ohio, that year. But, the Braves and the Dodgers decided to barnstorm together on their way north. They stopped to play games in cities like Mobile, New Orleans, and Birmingham. Before Henry ever got to Milwaukee, he had the chance to play in front of his family in Mobile, wearing a Braves uniform and sharing the field with Jackie Robinson.

I hope Daddy remembers what I told him when I was fourteen, Henry thought as his team warmed up. *I told him I'd be in the big leagues while Jackie Robinson was still there!*

11

ON SEPTEMBER 5, 1954, Henry broke his ankle sliding in to third base for a triple.

It was just like Bobby Thompson.

It meant he was out of baseball for the rest of the season. Henry went back home to Mobile.

After Henry got his cast off, he asked his brother, Tommie, to throw him change-ups—pitches that are slower than the usual pitches that are thrown. Tommie was only fifteen years old, but he worked with Henry at Carver Park in Mobile for the rest of the winter. Little did he and Henry imagine that they would both be on the same team in the big leagues some day. Even at fifteen, Tommie's change-up was good enough to get Henry ready for 1955.

Henry felt that he needed extra practice to get in shape for the season after having a cast on all winter. So, he reported early to spring training camp in Bradenton, Florida.

After he had been there for a couple of days, a manager for the team called out to him, "Hey, Henry, you've got a telegram."

Henry couldn't imagine who would be sending him a telegram at spring training. He was even more amazed when he read it! It was from the Commissioner of Baseball, Ford Frick. Frick told Henry that he was being fined for reporting early to spring training. Henry was shocked that there was a rule that prevented players from working extra hard.

Before the regular season began, Henry went to see Donald Davidson, the traveling secretary for the Braves.

"Donald, I'd like to have a number with two digits on it on my jersey," Henry said.

Davidson laughed and said, "You're too skinny to carry around two numbers. Besides, all the great players—Musial, DiMaggio, Ruth, and Gehrig—had single numbers. You should have one too."

"Donald, we got a letter from the commissioner saying that he would like for all of the outfielders to have double digit numbers. He wants all of the infielders to have single digits and the pitchers to have double digits but in the real low double digits."

Donald looked up from what is he was working

on. "OK, why don't you take 44?"

Henry smiled. "OK. That's what I'll have."

As it turned out, Henry hit forty-four home runs four different times in his career. After that happened, Davidson said, "I wish I had given him the number 66. What if he'd taken 66?"

Henry was named the Braves Most Valuable Player in 1955, and he earned $17,000.

Henry's baseball successes continued to mount, but the Braves did not come in first in 1956.

"If anything good came out of blowing the pennant (coming in second) in 1956," said Henry, "It was 1957. We didn't want it to happen again."

One of Henry's big goals in baseball was to win the Triple Crown. This meant being the player who would lead the league in batting average, runs batted in and home runs.

"I honestly didn't consider myself a home run hitter, but at the same time, I did think I had a chance to win a home run title," said Henry. "I just figured that if you hit the ball hard enough often enough, the home runs would start to pile up."

Henry's first good chance to win the Triple Crown was in 1957. The Braves won a lot of games early that season, and most days Henry was right in the middle of the action. By June, it looked like he had a good chance at the Triple Crown, and the Braves were favorites to come in first.

On September 23, they needed only one more win.

A sellout crowd of excited fans jammed into the stands of the new County Stadium in Milwaukee, Wisconsin. The Braves, were playing the St. Louis Cardinals. The winner of the game would be the champion of the National League.

As the Braves took the field to warm-up, the fans roared. Henry, the second youngest batting champion in the National League, was playing center field.

"When I have my timing," Hank said that day, "I can hit everyone. When I haven't, I can't hit anyone."

Many pitchers felt that even when his timing was off, that he could hit a baseball a mile. Even when swinging at what appeared to be a bad ball, Hank's wrists were so strong that he could wait until the last possible second to whip his bat around.

When Aaron came to the plate, he stood deep in the batter's box, gently waving his bat. He stood straight up, not crouching, and his eyes appeared half closed.

The crucial game for the championship seesawed

back and forth. The Cardinals scored two runs, then the Braves tied the game 2-2.

Whenever a game is tied after nine innings, the teams continue to play one inning at a time until one team scores more runs than the other.

The crowd went wild as the game moved into the tenth inning. No one scored, and the eleventh inning began. Henry would be the third batter.

The first batter hit a single. The second made an out.

Henry walked slowly to the plate. He gently wiggling his bat back and forth, watching the pitcher.

The pitcher looked back at Henry, standing there waiting for the first pitch, eyes half closed, bat slowly circling.

He chose a curve ball as his first pitch.

Henry Aaron lowered his right shoulder and whipped his bat around.

The crowd roared. The ball headed straight out toward center field. Higher and higher it soared while Wally Moon, the Cardinals center fielder, turned and ran toward the 402 feet sign. He leaped, but the ball was gone! Henry Aaron had hit his 43rd homerun for the season.

The crowd went wild! Fans were dancing up and down, hugging and patting each other on the back.

The Braves players were waiting for Henry at home plate. They lifted him onto their shoulders and carried him off of the field.

The Braves were the National League champions, and it was Henry Aaron's home run that had done it!

In the locker room, teammates, writers, cameramen, television and radio announcers mobbed Henry.

"Are you excited, Henry?" a reporter asked.

"Boy, am I excited!" Henry grinned.

"Were you ever as excited as this?"

"No, sir. This is the greatest thing that ever happened to me."

"Do you think this was your most important home run?"

"I don't just think so. I know it," he said without hesitating.

It might have been his most important that day, but even more important things were yet to come.

The Mauwaukee Braves went on to win the World Series that year over the mighty New York Yankees.

A few weeks later, Henry Aaron was named Most Valuable Player for the National League. Even for a twenty-three year old MVP, who had won his first World Series, there was more to life than baseball.

After the World Series, Mobile arranged to have

a Hank Aaron Day. Henry decided the only proper way to get there was aboard the L&N Hummingbird train. "It was like leaving town in an old beat-up Volkswagen and returning in a Rolls-Royce," Henry said.

As the train pulled into the station, a band played "Take Me Out to the Ball Game" and "On Mobile Bay." Henry and Barbara were put into a limousine and taken to the Colored Elks Club. Mayor Joseph Langan gave Henry a key to the city. Then, Henry was invited to speak to one of the white service clubs in Mobile.

"May I bring Barbara along?" Henry asked.

"This club is for men only," the club member said.

"Fine, I understand," Henry replied. "But how about if I bring my father? Daddy has never been to anything like that, and it will be a real treat for him."

The club member squirmed and stuttered. He cleared his throat and finally spoke, "We just can't allow that. It is one thing for a black World Series winner to speak to our club, but it is another thing to have his black Daddy sitting with all the white men in the audience."

Henry's bubble was burst.

He canceled the speech.

If his Daddy would not be allowed to go, Henry would not go either.

12

MEQUON, WISCONSIN, was a community just
north of Milwaukee—home of the Braves—and near
the shore of Lake Michigan.

It was there that Henry and Barbara bought their
first home, shortly after their first son, Henry Junior—
Hankie—was born.

The Aarons were just about the only black family
in Mequon. Most of the neighbors were friendly, but
there were times when they realized that they were
different from the people there.

One day Henry walked over to his neighbor's
yard. The neighbor's dog began to growl at him.

"Oh, I'm sorry," said the neighbor. "He's not used
to colored people."

Henry thought, *I wish that dogs were the only ones
around here who are not used to colored people.*

He realized that as far as he had come in baseball,
there was still a long way to go before black people

wouldn't be looked upon as "different".

That winter, nine months after Hankie was born, Barbara gave birth to twin boys, Gary and Lary. They were premature babies, and Gary died before they ever left the hospital. Lary was weak, and even after a few months, reports from the doctors weren't very good. Henry and Barbara decided that their infant son needed the warmer temperature and special touch that Mama had in Mobile. So, they took him to live with Estella. Even with his many baseball successes, Henry still had many hard personal decisions to make.

Finally, spring training arrived in 1958. Henry had a new car, a Chevrolet. Felix rode with him to spring camp in Bradenton, Florida.

They were not far from the city limits of Bradenton when a big Buick came up behind their car. The driver began bumping against the Chevrolet's rear bumper. Henry thought the driver wanted to pass, so he pulled over to let the car around. As the car sped by, he saw a crowd of white teenagers inside.

The Buick didn't continue along the highway. Instead, the driver slowed to a crawl, waiting to continue his dangerous game. Henry passed the slow moving car and the Buick rushed up behind him again. This time, the Buick's driver went into the other lane and veered sharply toward Henry's car.

"They ripped into the front of my car at sixty miles an hour," Henry recalled. "Felix and I went into a ditch, then bounced out and swerved into the highway, with cars speeding all around us."

Luckily, neither one was hurt. When they got to camp, Henry told teammates about it. "Don't mention it to the newspapermen," Henry was cautioned.

"I almost lost my life, and you want me to keep it a secret?" Henry asked. Henry did talk to the Milwaukee writers, and there were a couple of articles about what had happened. But, for the most part, the incident was ignored.

In Bradenton in 1958, the white players stayed at the big pink Manatee River Hotel and the black players lived in an apartment over a garage owned by a black school teacher named Lulu Gibson. Each year, one player got to live in a room in the main house. They called it "big house" privileges. The rest of the players shared two bedrooms and a hallway. Even though it was crowded, it was clean, and the meals that Mrs. Gibson and her sister cooked were wonderful. But it wasn't the Manatee River Hotel.

Even if he could not change the way black people

were treated, Henry continued to show America that black players were needed in baseball. The Milwaukee Braves won the league championship in 1958. Even though they lost the World Series to the Yankees, Henry was a champion. He had thirty home runs, batted .326, and won his first Gold Glove Award, given only to the players who play the very best in the field. He was in third place for the Most Valuable Player vote. He would never again play in a World Series or win another Most Valuable Player Award. He didn't realize how many changes were about to take place for him in baseball.

"It seemed like we spent most of those years laughing or fighting. And winning. And having our hearts broken. They were happy days that should have been a little happier and lasted a little longer," Henry said. "At the time, it never occurred to us that they would be over when the fifties ended. We were too good and too cocky to believe that."

One thing that changed Henry in 1959 was a new made-for-television show called *Home Run Derby*. Several players each week were selected to hit home runs. Whoever hit the most was the winner, and kept coming back on the show as long as he won. Every show gave the winner a chance to earn more money.

"I ended up hitting more home runs and winning more money than anybody," Henry recalled. "I took home about $30,000, which was almost two years worth of salaries, and used it to buy my parents a grocery store in Toulminville."

This chance to earn more money changed Henry's way of thinking. "Home run hitters made the money. I noticed that they never had a show called Singles Derby." Henry Aaron was becoming a home run hitter.

By 1962, Henry's salary was up to about $50,000 a year. He thought that was more than he needed for his family's lifestyle in Wisconsin. His family had been accepted in Mequon. He was pleased with his home. The patio was shaped like a baseball field with a fence around it, benches for the bullpen, and a barbecue pit in the center. He and his family spent a lot of time at home watching westerns on their new color television or barbecuing. On Henry's birthday of that year, his baby daughter, Dorinda, was born.

As he watched his children grow up, he began preaching the same advice to them that his mother preached to him.

He preached about appreciating the good things of life that they had, not being proud or cocky, and of getting an education.

Henry's fame had come from his ability to catch, throw and, especially, hit a baseball, not from being a great student. Now that he was older, he knew that he was one of a lucky few who had been able to do it.

He had seen hundreds of other young men try and fail.

When his children wanted to challenge him about the need for an education to get ahead, he was quick with his response: "I'm Hank Aaron, and you're not," Henry would say. He didn't mean it to brag. He meant that the children would have to learn to make their own way in life.

He also reminded his children that his life as a baseball player wouldn't last forever. "Just remember, I could break something and never play again," he kept telling them.

"The only thing you have to fall back on is your education," he said. "Remember, you can always fall off the same ladder that you climbed up on."

Henry's home was a busy place. It was always filled with friends or relatives. Henry and Barbara felt right at home in Mequon. It was so pleasant there with dairy cows in the pastures and foxes in the meadows. They didn't realize that even more change was about to happen in their lives.

The Braves—"The Miracle of Milwaukee," as they were called—were no longer drawing big crowds. Like the hula hoop or ducktail haircuts, they seemed to be a fad from the fifties. Attendance at ball games kept dropping. Even though Henry and the team kept playing well, the fans didn't seem to care.

In 1963, Henry came the closest he ever would to the Triple Crown. He hit forty-four home runs, hit the most runs batted in, and his batting average was only seven points behind Tommy Davis of the Dodgers. He finished first in runs.

In 1965, the Braves had a good chance to win the league championship. Henry and Eddie Mathews set a record for the most home runs by teammates. Nobody in Milwaukee seemed to care. Only a few thousand people showed up for the last few games of the season.

Two days before the season ended, Henry hit a home run.

It was exciting, but not *that* exciting. Henry had hit a lot of home runs that year.

Little did the Milwaukee fans realize, but that would be the last home run that they would see for a while. The Milwaukee Braves were about to become the first team ever to leave a city without baseball.

13

ATLANTA STADIUM had been built before anyone even had an idea that the Braves would be coming there. It was built as a magnet for a professional baseball team to come to Atlanta.

Atlanta was all the things that Milwaukee no longer was—a hopeful city that was the center of a thousand smaller towns.

The Milwaukee Braves were now the Atlanta Braves. The ball club had moved.

Henry was thirty-two years old. He no longer was the skinny kid who was all wrists and forearms. He felt like he was starting over and he wanted to do it with style.

"The first time I took batting practice in Atlanta-Fulton County Stadium, I knew that my career was headed in a new direction." Henry said. "Atlanta was the highest city in the major leagues, as well as the hottest, and if you could get the ball into the air, there was a good chance that it wouldn't come down in the playing field. I thought when I first saw it that it was a place I could do a lot of damage in. I thought I could hit a lot of home runs if I played to my potential."

By the first day of summer, Henry had hit twenty-four home runs, which tied a major-league record.

However, Henry didn't feel that he was a popular player in Atlanta. A reporter interviewed him when the announcement came that the Braves were moving there. The reporter asked, "What are your plans? Are you planning to move to Atlanta?"

"No, I'm not planning on moving to Atlanta," Henry replied. "I'm going to stay right here in Milwaukee where my kids are in school. I think that I deserve to keep them in school."

"Hank doesn't want to come to Atlanta" sports pages read. It wasn't what Henry meant at all. Even though Henry knew the reports were wrong, he decided to just leave it alone and go about his usual quiet way. He was looking forward to coming to Atlanta to play. But, because of all of the news comments, instead of leaving his family in Milwaukee, he decided to go ahead and bring them to Atlanta with him.

"This was one of the greatest things that ever

happened to me, coming to Atlanta," Henry said. "I was close to Mobile, where I could get to see my parents, my friends.

More and more people started to talk about Henry's gift for hitting home runs. Furman Bisher, a well-known sports writer for the *Atlanta Journal-Constitution*, was the first one in Atlanta to suggest that Henry might have a chance to break Babe Ruth's record.

In August 1968, Henry was the first player to be honored by having his own night in Atlanta Stadium. He had just hit his 500th home run. Henry was nervous at the ceremony. He stepped up to the microphone and dropped his hat. Both Henry and Braves owner Bill Bartholomay bent down to pick it up. They bumped into each other and knocked over the microphone. Henry had to laugh because it reminded him of a night long ago in Jacksonville when he had been honored and had dropped dollar bills all over the field. He felt he was much better at hitting the ball than he was at talking about it.

Henry's batting routine became a familiar sight in Atlanta Stadium. He would carry his bat in one hand and his helmet in the other. He would stop just outside the batter's box, balance his bat on his thigh, put on his helmet with both hands and stare at the pitcher.

Then, when he stepped to home plate he would twist his spikes into the deep part of the batter's box, wave his bat over the plate in two or three circles, cock his right arm, and wait for the right pitch. When it arrived, Henry would turn his hips, snap his wrists, and raise his eyes, never looking to see if he had hit a home run. He would lope around the bases with his head straight, shoulders back, and elbows swinging at his sides. Fans could hardly wait for Henry to bat.

During the 1970 season, Henry hit the first home run that ever landed in the left-field upper deck of Atlanta Stadium. The Braves painted a gold hammer on the seat that marked the spot. Henry also hit another high point that year. He got his 3,000th hit in baseball. At that time, there were only eight other players who had reached that mark. Henry was featured on the cover of *Sports Illustrated* magazine.

Henry put a lot of energy into the home run race. He spent more time at the ballpark than he did at home. The more that Barbara complained about the situation, the more Henry stayed away. Finally, Barbara filed for a divorce. By February 1971, his marriage had ended and Henry moved to the Landmark Apartments in downtown Atlanta. Henry still spent time at the house a lot so that he could be with his children.

In 1971, Henry was thirty-seven years old. At an age when many players retired from baseball, he was hitting more home runs than ever. There wasn't one month that season that Henry didn't hit at least seven home runs. By the end of the season, he had forty-seven home runs, the most he ever hit in one season.

The chase was on to become the Home Run King.

Henry continued to earn many baseball awards. Midway through the 1972 season, he hit home run number 660. This broke Babe Ruth's record for home runs hit by a player with one team. Then, in September 1972, Henry broke Stan Musial's record for total bases. Total bases means adding up the number of bases for each hit, with a single being one, a double being two, a triple being three, and a home run being four. "If there is any one record that I think best represents what I was all about as a hitter, that's the one," Henry said. "As far as I was concerned, the object of batting was to hit the ball and get as many bases as possible."

In spite of the successes, Henry wasn't happy.

"For a while there, Hank was as sad and lonesome as any man I ever saw," remembered his teammate, Dusty Baker. "It made me sad just to see him that way. Before the divorce, when Ralph Garr and I first came up to the Braves, Hank and Barbara more or less adopted us. We'd be over at their house for dinner almost every night. Then, all of a sudden, Hank was alone."

Things were about to change.

One morning, Henry was supposed to appear on an Atlanta television talk show called "Today in Georgia." The co-hostess, Billye Williams, had contacted him. She explained that she would be doing a series of stories about Braves players called "Billye at the Bat." Henry was supposed to be the first Brave on the show.

At nine o'clock on the day Henry was scheduled to appear, there was no Henry! At nine forty-five, he still was not there. It was embarrassing to Billye and to her show. But, they decided to reschedule him. The next time that Henry was supposed to appear, Billye stopped by the Landmark Apartments on her way to work.

"I stopped by to see if he was up," Billye remembered. "The Braves had played...the night before, and I knew that he might still be sleeping. So I kind of leaned on the doorbell until he answered."

Henry finally came to the door. Billye offered to drive him to the studio.

"No, I promise I'll be there as soon as I am dressed," Henry said.

Henry was good to his word. After he appeared on the show, he promised to help Billye to arrange to get other players to appear on the show.

They started to talk on the telephone quite a bit. Henry thought that she was very sophisticated and charming. She was also a wonderful mother to her little girl, Ceci. Billye had all of the education that Henry did not.

"She helped bring me into the world of books and ideas," Henry later said. "At the same time, I made her a baseball fan, although she would have me believe that she went to the games for the hot dogs and peanuts."

Henry was happier than he had been in a long time.

He continued to play baseball and to hit home runs. His 700th career home run came in Atlanta on July 21, 1973.

"I was affected in a lot of ways by reaching 700," Henry remembered. "There was something about getting there that made me feel I was almost at my destination, like I had been traveling the back roads for twenty years, and suddenly I was on Ruth's street, turning onto his driveway."

Henry wanted to tie Babe Ruth's record of 714 home runs during the 1973 season. He didn't want it to hang over his head through the winter.

He had other plans that winter—mainly, to marry Billye Williams. He hated the idea of coming so close at the end of the season and not making it.

It was not to be. Henry hit his 713th home run and not another that season.

Babe Ruth still had the record.

There was a happy and surprising moment before the season ended. When Henry reached left field for the ninth inning, fans there stood up and applauded. Then the fans around third base stood up to applaud. Then the fans behind home plate, and right field, and the upper deck. Almost 40,000 fans stood and cheered for Henry for five minutes.

"There have been a lot of standing ovations for a lot of baseball players, but this was one for the ages as far as I was concerned." Henry said. "I couldn't believe that I was Hank Aaron and this was Atlanta, Georgia. I don't think I'd ever felt so good in my life.

"I wasn't ready for it. I didn't know how to respond to something like that, because it had never come up before."

It was something that Henry would have to get used to.

14

HENRY HAD PLENTY TO THINK ABOUT during the off-season in 1973.

He and Billye married in a small ceremony in Jamaica on November 12. Even though they tried to keep the wedding quiet, they didn't have much of a private honeymoon. The wedding made the newspapers and reporters were around.

Laying on the beach in Jamaica with his bride, Henry would think about what lay ahead for him in the 1974 season.

If he stayed healthy, he surely would become the baseball player to hit more home runs that any other player.

He would break the record held so long by the great Babe Ruth.

Sometimes he would think about what he and Babe Ruth had in common other than home runs. They both had played for the Braves. Their fathers both ran neighborhood taverns. They both left high school early to start playing baseball.

The one big difference was that Henry was black and Babe Ruth was white.

Almost every day someone reminded him of it. And it usually was not in a nice way.

As he threatened Babe Ruth's record, he was threatened, too. Hate mail pored in with threats that he would be killed and that his children would be kidnapped. Henry's secretary, Carla Koplin, was going through almost 3,000 letters a day. Some had to be turned over to the FBI because of the threats.

One morning when Henry and Billye were eating breakfast, FBI agents came to their house with a report that Henry's oldest daughter, Gaile, a student at Fisk University in Nashville, had been kidnapped.

It turned out not to be true, but frightening nonetheless.

Even with extra protection, Henry, Billye, and Barbara were worried. Ceci, Billye's daughter, whom Henry had adopted when he and Billye married, lived at home with them. Henry's other kids were living with Barbara and going to private schools in Atlanta. The schools were strict about keeping strangers and visitors away from the children. Once, the newspaper ran a picture of Henry and Dorinda at a Braves father-kid game. Somebody clipped the picture and sent it to Henry with the words, "Daddy, please think about us. Please, please!" People even called Henry's mother and father in Mobile and told them that they would never see their boy again.

Henry tried not to take the threats too seriously, but they were always in the back of his mind.

"I was just a man doing something that God had given me the power to do," Henry said. "And, I was living like an outcast in my own country. I had no-where to go except home and to the ballpark, home and to the ballpark."

When fans learned through newspaper stories about all the threats and hate mail, thousands of people started writing positive letters to Henry.

Dear Mr. Aaron,

I am twelve years old, and I wanted to tell you that I have read many articles about the prejudice against you. I really think it's bad.

I don't care what color you are. You could be green and it wouldn't matter. These nuts that keep comparing you in every way to Ruth are dumb. Maybe he's better. Maybe you are. How can you compare two people 30 or 40 years apart? You can't really. So many

*things are different. It's just some people can't stand to
see someone a bit different from them ruin something
someone else more like them set. I've never read where
you said you're better than Ruth. That's because you
never said it! What do those fans want you to do?*

Just quit hitting?

Newspaper reporters still compared Henry and
Babe Ruth. Henry had batted so many more times than
Ruth; Henry played with a livelier ball. Babe Ruth had
been a pitcher for part of his career; pitchers had been
better in Ruth's time. Travel was tougher in Ruth's
time. Ruth had a higher batting average. Like weeds,
the comparisons kept popping up.

The press always surrounded Henry. The last time
a player had been through something like Henry was
going through was when Roger Maris broke Babe
Ruth's single season home run record in 1961. Roger
Maris was like Henry in some ways. He was a very
private person who did not enjoy publicity.

Henry was anxious for it all to end.

15

1974.

This was Henry Aaron's year to break the home run record that so many had said was unbreakable.

It was the year that Henry would pass the great Babe Ruth.

When baseball season began that April, he had to hit only two home runs to break the record.

Since Henry played for the Braves, a lot of people wanted him to hit the record-breaking home run in Atlanta.

But the Braves started that season April 4 against the Reds in Cincinnati, Ohio. Eddie Mathews, manager of the Braves, was one of the ones who wanted Henry to break the record in Atlanta.

He wanted it so much that he decided not to play Henry until the team came back to Atlanta from Cincinnati.

Some sportswriters protested.

The Commissioner of Baseball, Bowie Kuhn, ordered the Braves to play Henry, whether he felt like it or not, in at least two of the three games against the Reds.

Opening day was cold and damp. Henry got to the ballpark early for a press conference, then went straight to the clubhouse. He was not in a good mood.

The great civil rights leader, Dr. Martin Luther King, had died on this date five years earlier. Henry wanted a moment of silence to be observed before the game in Dr. King's memory.

Commissioner Kuhn refused, and wouldn't even talk to Henry about it.

"I should have known better," Henry said later. "If nothing else, though, I got the message across that we should be more concerned with Dr. King's legacy and less with Babe Ruth's. I was doing my best to keep things in perspective."

Dusty Baker came over to Henry. "Supe,"—Baker and Garr and some of the other players had started calling Henry that, short for Superstar—"You playing today, brother?"

Ralph Garr came up next. "We'll sure be glad when you get this thing over with."

Dusty nodded. He remembered a day the year before when Henry told him and Ralph not to sit next to him in the dugout in Atlanta.

"Why not?" Dusty had wanted to know.

"I've gotten a death threat that somebody in a red coat is going to shoot me and I don't want you in the way," Henry confided.

"Hank, we're down with you man, we ain't going nowhere," Dusty had bravely replied. But the whole game he and Ralph kept looking around for a guy in a red coat.

"Yes, Supe, we are ready for this to be over," Dusty agreed.

"I'll do it today," Henry promised.

The first inning wasn't over when Henry had his first chance to bat. Jack Billingham was the Reds' pitcher, and he was as nervous as Henry. He already had let two Braves players on base.

"I knew Billingham would throw me sinking fast balls, trying to get me to hit into a double play," Henry later analyzed about the tricky pitches that drop when they get close to home plate. "I was always a guess hitter, but, like most of my guesses, this one was an informed guess, based on my own history, and based on the pitcher's. I decided to wait for the sinker."

Henry did not swing at any of the first four pitches. Three of them were balls and one was a strike.

The next pitch came in low and fast. It was a sinker. Just as Henry had suspected.

Henry swung the bat, fast and hard. With his first swing of the 1974 season, the ball flew just high enough and far enough to drop over the fence. Henry hit the 714th home run of his career.

He had tied the record. Just like he promised.

Henry managed to keep calm as he trotted around the bases except that his eyes were damp with tears and he made it around a little faster than usual. "I just wanted to find home plate somewhere in the middle of the mob that was waiting there, because when I did, the long, excruciating chase would at last be over," Henry said. "I still had one more home run to go to set the record, but for the first time in several long years, I wasn't chasing anybody. It was like I had landed on the moon. I was there. All I had to do now was take the next step. From that point on, every home run I hit would set an all-time record."

Henry touched home plate and was touched in return by the reaction of the great Cincinnati catcher, Johnny Bench. Bench congratulated Henry as soon as his foot touched the plate, and then he moved away quickly as a swarm of Braves grabbed Henry. "What I remember is that everybody was right there celebrating with me, as if my record was their record, too. A player can't ask for anymore than that," Henry said.

Henry went to the stands and hugged Billye and his father. Gerald Ford, Vice President of the United States, and Bowie Kuhn, the Commissioner of Baseball, came onto the field and shook Henry's hand.

As soon as the game was over, he called his daughter, Ceci, to share his excitement with her.

Maybe now, finally, all the press conferences, questions, challenges and threats would be over.

But they weren't.

During a press conference after the game, Eddie Mathews announced that he wasn't going to play Henry in the next two games, which were to be played in Cincinnati. Eddie wanted Henry to break the record in Atlanta.

The Commissioner announced that the Braves had to play Henry in one of the two games. The uproar had started again. Henry sat out the next game on Saturday. The Commissioner threatened Eddie with suspension if he didn't let Henry play on Sunday.

So, Henry played on Sunday. He batted three times, struck out twice and grounded out once. By this point in the game, the Braves were ahead, so Eddie took Henry out.

After the game, some sportswriters wondered if Henry had not hit a home run on purpose.

"I had too much pride in my ability and too much respect for the integrity of the game to make an out on purpose," Henry said. "I'm glad I didn't break the record on the road, but it wasn't for any lack of effort."

It seemed that no matter what Henry did someone was always there to complain or to criticize. Henry was in a bad mood by the time he got back to Atlanta, but Atlanta was in a good mood. The annual Dogwood Festival was going on, and the Braves had planned a big "Hank Aaron Night" for the home opening game on Monday, April 8. Nearly 54,000 people came to the ballpark that night. There were balloons and marching bands. There was a program before the game that included a lot of Henry's old friends from all over the country.

It seemed to take forever to get the game started. Finally, Pearl Bailey sang the National Anthem. Henry's father, Herbert, threw out the first pitch.

Then, the Braves took the field against the Los Angeles Dodgers.

The Dodgers pitcher was Al Downing. He had been pitching for a number of years and was very good. He knew exactly what he was going to do to try to keep Henry from getting a hit.

Henry's first chance to bat came in the second inning.

He stood as close as he could to home plate, hoping that it would make Downing throw the ball to the opposite side of the plate. Henry knew that Downing was trying to out-think him.

Henry knew he would have to be patient and wait for just the right pitch.

Downing walked Henry on four straight balls.

Henry scored when Dusty Baker hit a double.

Nobody seemed to know when Henry crossed home plate that he broke Willie Mays' National League record for runs scored and put him in third place all time behind Ty Cobb and Babe Ruth. That was not the reason this crowd had come to the ball park that night.

Henry didn't come up to bat again until the fourth inning.

There were two outs and Darrell Evans, another Braves player, was on first base. The Dodgers were ahead, 3-1, and Henry knew that Downing wouldn't walk him. The score was too close. Downing was going to use every trick he had to get Henry out.

Henry walked toward home plate. He carried his bat in one hand and his helmet in the other. He stopped just outside the batter's box, balanced his bat on his thigh, put on his helmet with both hands and stared at Downing. Then, Henry twisted his spikes into the deep part of the batter's box, waved his bat over the plate in two or three circles, cocked his right arm, and waited for the right pitch.

What an important pitch it would be!

Downing's first pitch was a change-up that was so low it landed in the dirt. The umpire, Satch Davidson, threw that dirty ball out, and the first-base umpire, Frank Pulli, tossed Downing another one of the specially marked infrared balls. All of the balls that were pitched to Henry were marked so that they could be recovered when he hit a home run.

Downing rubbed the ball a little. Then he threw a slider. He wanted the ball to look like a strike to Henry, but then to slide sideways through the air and away from Henry's bat.

When a pitcher throws a slider just right, the batter will swing just about every time. And, just about every time the batter will miss. But sometimes, if the pitcher doesn't do everything just right, the slider doesn't slide. It just comes straight.

That is what happened on this pitch. Downing must have known that he had made a terrible mistake even before the ball reached the plate.

The slider wasn't sliding. It was low and down the middle!

And that was just fine with Henry.

Milo Hamilton, the Braves announcer said:

> *"Here's the pitch by*
> *Downing...Swinging...There's a drive*
> *into left-center field. That ball is gonna beee......*
> *OUTA HERE! IT'S GONE! IT'S 715!*
> *There's a new home run champion of all time!*
> *And it's Henry Aaron! The fireworks are going!*
> *Henry Aaron is coming around third! His team*
> *mates are at home plate.*
> *Listen to this crowd..."*

Henry in classic on-deck pose

For the first time ever, Henry watched the ball to see where it was going. He saw Dodger outfielder Bill Buckner run to the wall like he was going to catch it. Buckner turned and jumped, but the ball just kept going. Henry was as surprised as Buckner was.

Henry got to first base and thought, *I am the all time home run king of baseball.* Steve Garvey, the Dodgers' first baseman, shook Henry's hand as he passed the base. As Henry neared second, Davey Lopes, the second baseman, stuck out his hand.

Henry never remembered if he shook Davey's hand or not because about that time two college students came out of nowhere and started to run beside Henry and pound him on the back. Henry hardly noticed them.

"I was in my own little world at the time," Henry said later. "It was like I was running in a bubble and I could see all these people jumping up and down and waving their arms in slow motion."

For once, Henry had a big smile on his face as he came around third base. As he ran to home plate, Ralph Garr grabbed his leg and tried to force it onto the plate. Ralph screamed, "Touch it, Supe! Just touch it!"

As soon as Henry touched the plate, his team-mates mobbed him. Somehow, through the crowd Estella found her son. She grabbed Henry in a big bear hug.

"Good Lord, I didn't know Mama was that strong," Henry said. "I thought she was going to squeeze the life out of me."

About that time, Tom House, a young relief pitcher who had been warming up in the Braves bullpen came sprinting in with the ball.

"Hammer, here it is!" he shouted as he stuck the ball in Henry's hand.

The game stopped. There was a ceremony to honor Henry. When he stepped up to the microphone he said exactly what he felt: "Thank God it's over."

Henry came up to bat again during the game. It was at that moment it hit him that the whole thing was over– all of the threats and all of the worry and all of the pressure. When he walked to the on-deck circle, where players stand right before it is their turn to bat, Ralph Garr shouted, "Come on, Supe, break Hank Aaron's record."

That night, when Henry got home, he got down on his knees and closed his eyes and thanked God for pulling him through the past twenty-five years of baseball.

"I felt a deep sense of gratitude and a wonderful surge of freedom all at the same time," Henry said. "I also felt a stream of tears running down my face."

Epilogue

EVENTUALLY, HENRY AARON broke the record that he set on April 8, 1974, but not that night.

Henry finished the season in Atlanta with 733 home runs.

Then, his old friend, Bud Selig hired him to return to Milwaukee and play with the Brewers. There he broke Henry Aaron's record twenty-two more times. Henry Aaron ended his career with 755 home runs. He also had 2,297 runs batted in, which was another record.

Many people think that Henry Aaron didn't enjoy his baseball years, or that he is bitter about the experience. When he hears such comments, Henry says, "There is no one in the world I would rather be than Henry Louis Aaron. But I am a realist. I have eyes and ears to see and hear what is wrong, and I have a mouth to express my feelings about what is wrong."

Henry will always remember the terrible names that he was called. He will remember how he was refused service in restaurants and hotels. Most of all, he will remember that his life was threatened because he had the nerve to challenge Babe Ruth's record.

None of those memories change his opinion about baseball.

"I love baseball, always did and always will," Henry says. "I love the essence of the game, the contest between the pitcher and the hitter. I love the variety of skills the game demands, arm strength and leg strength, the ability to run and throw and hit and think. I think I owe everything I have to the game of baseball."

"I know that most people, when they think of me, think of home runs or, if they really know the game, think of 755," he said. But what I would most like them to remember about me is not the home runs, or the hits or the runs batted in, but that I was concerned about the well being of other people. I'd like for people to understand that I have a very deep passion for kids. I love young people."

After his retirement from baseball, Ted Turner, the new owner of the Atlanta Braves, hired Henry to work in the Braves' business office. He continues to work as senior vice-president for the Atlanta Braves. Henry Aaron also works for people and causes just as quietly and behind the scenes as he played baseball. Through the Henry Aaron Scholarship Program and his own foundation, Chasing the Dream, Henry has helped to raise millions of dollars to help young people.

"Through Chasing the Dream, we've encouraged youngsters to take chances, to explore opportunities, to try to become the greatest pianist in the world or the greatest schoolteacher or the greatest accountant," Henry says. This organization helps children between the ages of 9-12.

Henry has also continued to be involved with the Boy Scouts. He is the 2001 governor for the state of Georgia for the Boys and Girls Club.

"He gives back to the community," said baseball great Ted Williams. "Community, that's a two-dollar word for people. Hank Aaron cares about kids and people and cares about doing what he thinks is right. You see, Hank Aaron works for people and causes just the way he played baseball– without a lot of noise."

"Then, before you know it, there's Hank stepping across home plate. Making a difference. Standing up for what he believes in."

Henry modestly says, "It was passed down to me by my mother, whose life revolved around the church, and by my father, who was a good man.

"I was a Boy Scout when I was a child, and in a way, I've always lived by the Boy Scout motto—trying to be kind, loyal, brave, clean, obedient, all those simple virtues."

Many people think of Henry Aaron as a hero.

"Am I a hero?" he asks. "I suppose I am to some people. If I am, I hope it's not only for my home runs, for my physical accomplishments on the baseball field. I hope it's also for my beliefs, my stands, my opinions."

"I'm not at ease being a hero. Heroes, I feel, should be people you see on an everyday basis. Your parents. Your teachers."

Henry surrounded by his family; wife Billye to his immediate left

Roz Morris
Henry Louis Aaron

1934 Born on February 5 in Mobile, Alabama

1942 Moves to nearby Toulminville

1950 Joins the Mobile Black Bears baseball team

1952 Joins the Indianapolis Clowns
Wins Northern League's Rookie of the Year Award

1953 Assigned by the Milwaukee Braves to the
Jacksonville Tars of the South Atlantic (Sally) League
Named Sally League's Most Valuable Player
Marries Barbara Lucas October 6

1954 First daughter, Gaile, is born
Hits first major league home run April 12

1955 Makes first appearance at the All-Star Game
Named Braves Most Valuable Player

1956 Wins first National League batting title

1957 First son, Hankie, is born
Hits 100th career home run on August 15

Henry Aaron: Dream Chaser

Hits first World Series home run on October 5

Named National League's Most Valuable Player

Sons Gary and Lary are born

1958 Wins first Gold Glove award

Plays in second World Series

1959 Wins second batting title

Appears on "Home Run Derby"

1960 Hits 200th career home run on July 3

1962 Daughter, Dorinda, is born

1963 Hits 300th career home run on April 19th

Wins second home run crown

1965 Hits last home run by a Milwaukee Braves
player in Milwaukee County Stadium on September 20

1966 Hits 400th career home run on April 20

Wins third home run crown and fourth runs-
batted-in title

1967 Wins fourth home run crown

Roz Morris

1968 Hits 500th career home run on July 14

1971 Hits 600th career home run on April 27

1972 Moves into 2nd place on all-time home run list on June 10
Sets all-time record for most total bases (6,135) September 2

1973 Hits 700th career home run July 21
Marries Billye Williams November 12

1974 Ties all-time home run record (714) April 4
Hits career home run number 715 April 8
Traded to Milwaukee Brewers November 2

1975 Sets runs-batted-in record (2,212) May 1

1976 Hits last home run of career (755) on July 20
Becomes player development director for Atlanta Braves

1982 Inducted into Baseball Hall of Fame

1990 Becomes senior vice-president and assistant to president of Atlanta Braves

About the Author

Roz Morris has taught students from preschool
through eighth grade. She currently teaches third grade
at Shades Mountain Elementary School in Hoover,
Alabama. Mrs. Morris holds an M.Ed. in Elementary
Education from the University of Georgia, and is certi-
fied to teach grades K through 8. She is a member of
the Alabama Geographic Alliance, the state board of
the Alabama Council for Teachers of English, and the
1999-2000 Alabama Textbook Committee for Language
Arts.